WRR
N
6853
1M33
NSY
2067

oooh!
MATISSE

LIBRARY
FRANKLIN PIERCE UNIVERSITY
RINDGE, NH 03461

Love and merci to:
Olivia, Hannah, Lance, parents,
Michel & Tom, George Greenfield,
and most of all, the Matisse family,
for your trust and for letting us share Henri Matisse
in bold new ways.

oooh!
MATISSE

Mil Niepold & Jeanyves Verdu

TRICYCLE PRESS
Berkeley | Toronto

WHAT IS THIS?

**yellow,
I am
the
sun**

and blue, i am the fingers

that shield my eyes

yellow,
I am
the sand
and blue,
I am
a feather
on the
shore

oooh!

I AM A LEAF

AND THIS, WHAT IS THIS?

white,
I am snow

*and blue, I am
the mountains below*

white, I am the tail of a

and blue, I am

whale

the ocean around her

oooh!

I AM
A DOVE

WHAT IS THIS?

white,
I am
a splash
of milk

and green,
I am the rug
that soaks it up

white,
I am
a shining
light

**and green,
I am
the grass**

oooh!

I AM
A STAR

AND THIS?

pink, I am love

and white, I am the path to it

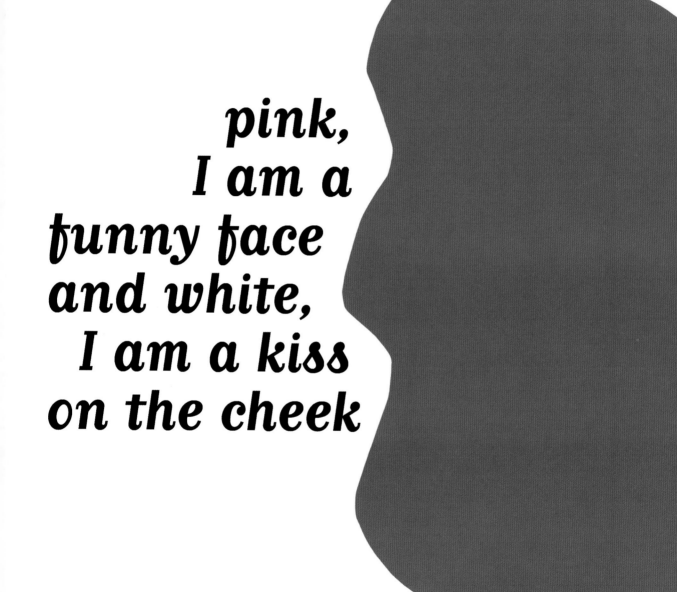

pink,
I am a
funny face
and white,
I am a kiss
on the cheek

oooh!

I AM
A FLOWER

AND WHAT ARE THESE?

white,
I am a note
to put in
a bottle

and yellow,
I am the bottle
floating in a
black sea

yellow,
I am
a ray of light

and white,
I am a rabbit
in a dark hole

oooh!

I AM
A GUITAR

(ARE THOSE YOUR HANDS?)

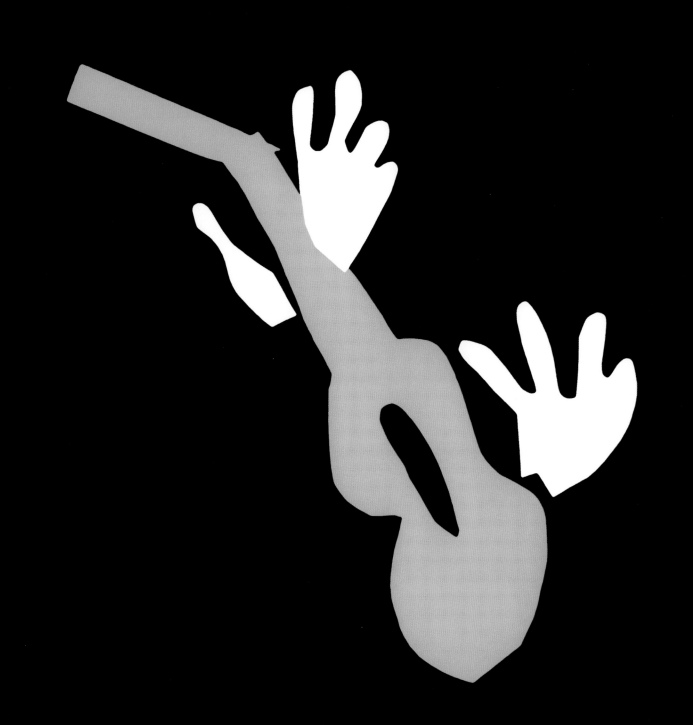

oooh!

THANK YOU MISTER MATISSE!

1

Back cover of the
book "Chapelle
du Rosaire des
Dominicaines
de Vence par
Henri Matisse"
/ 1951 /
Photo: Archives
Matisse, Paris

2

Flower / Fleur

Gouache on paper
/ 1952-1953 /
Photo: Archives
Matisse, Paris

3

The Sadness of
the King
/ La Tristesse
du Roi
/ 1952 /
Cutout.
Inv. AM 3279 P.
Photo: Philippe Migeat.
MNAM, Paris

4

**Birds /
Les Oiseaux**
*Gouache on paper
/ 1947 /
Photo: Private
collection*

5

**Cover of Verve
issue 13**
*Lithographic
reproduction
of gouache on paper
/ 1945 /
Photo: Archives
Matisse, Paris*

Text and illustrations copyright © 2007 by Jeanyves Verdu and Mil Niepold
All works of Henri Matisse © 2007 Succession H. Matisse / Artists Rights Society, NY

All rights reserved. No part of this book may be reproduced in any form without the written permission of the publisher,
except in the case of brief quotations embodied in critical articles or reviews.

Tricycle Press
an imprint of Ten Speed Press
PO Box 7123
Berkeley, California 94707
www.tricyclepress.com

Design by Jeanyves Verdu
Typeset in CircusMouse-Deco, Matrix script, Conduit

Library of Congress Cataloging-in-Publication Data

Niepold, Mil.
  Ooh! Matisse : a book / by Mil Niepold and Jean-Yves Verdu.
    p. cm.
  ISBN-13: 978-1-58246-227-1
  ISBN-10: 1-58246-227-5
  1. Matisse, Henri, 1869-1954--Juvenile literature. 2. Picture books for
children. I. Verdu, Jean-Yves. II. Title.
  N6853.M33N54 2007
  759.4--dc22
                                    2006102319

First Tricycle Press printing, 2007
Printed in China
1 2 3 4 5 6 — 12 11 10 09 08 07

Franklin Pierce University

00176518

DUE